TWIN TAN DOGS, OBEDIENCE & DISCIPLINE

A Modern Mystical Bestiary

by

LYNN STRONGIN

Credits:
Cricket on-line Review first published the title poem in Autumn, 2007.
"O mice who have been to the Fine Arts museum" originally appeared in "Ghoti" on-line; "Short Visiting Hours for Children" and "Petronius" first appeared in *Prairie Schooner* and *New Works Review*. "If we speak a river language" first appeared in another form in *Alba,* and "Cider Apples" first appeared in *Prism International*.

Cover:
A portion from *The Fate of The Animals,* by Franz Marc (1913); in the public domain

© 2010, Lynn Strongin
Ravenna Press

First Edition

ISBN: 978-0-9822115-9-5
LCCN: 2010941857

ravennapress.com
Spokane, Washington, USA

For cousin Jerry Wayne Slater

Table of Contents:

Part One

Look After My Animals, 1
What animals came, 2
Frost on Roots, 3
When the waterfowl put their heads together. 4
The Brightness of Toy, 5
Audition, 7
Braiding her hair in morning, 8
Mice who have been to the first arts museum in Boston, 9
Federico's Lamb, 10
The Six-sided Snowflake, 13
The Long Brown Body of the Street is Dying, 14
Portraits go dark on Audubon wallpaper, 15
Black Swans, White Swans, 16
Burst of Sparrow Like Gunfire, 17
50th anniversary of *Krystalnacht*, 18
Danish Geese in Dutch Museum, 19
A Pensioner, 20
Goose-White, Moon-Bright, 21
She loves her animals, 22
It's a rambutan, 23

Part Two

Fish Blow Ashore, 27
I am going out, 28
His Paws Smell of Soap, 29
Hydrocephalic child with wood & metal zoological garden, 30
Cider Apples, 31
She writes me a letter while she's strapped to the chemo chair, 32
Something Very Quiet, 33
Sonnets for Cyan (Cygnet—swan), 37
The Owl Italicized, 40
Christina's World, 41
Martha's Yard, 42

Horsefall Slow Motion, Reversed, 45
Buckled, 47
Mad Dog Winter, 48
Writing by Lightning, 49
Dark Tea, 50
We take the plunge, 51
Animals Eating Ice, 53
Diamond, Black Swan, Black Sun, Drifting, 55
We cannot stop of the bird of the past from singing, 56

Part Three

I saw them sitting one round wood table:, 59
Happiness Doesn't Matter, 60
Butterfly Collector, 63
Triangular Triage took time, 64
Bee Colony Collapse, 65
Never let me go, 66
Bird Calls echo back &, 67
Mystery House, 68
Snowgeese, 71
You carried many keys, 72
Avatar (Apiary), 73
It would be lovely to hear from you in the old-fashioned way, 74
If we speak a river language, 75
Twin tan dogs, 76
15h Drawbridge, 77
Mud Fields of Passchendaele, 78
Never to Forgive, 80
Boy with Ball, 81
Trampled in one of the last stampedes of the century, 83
Why are we thinking of an afterlife?, 84
Fragile X, 85

Part One

Animalia Passicaglia

Look After My Animals

    The fast the slow, the tall & low the tallow
        milk with silver flaws of flowers nib on parchment, yellow.
        Those with cleft hoof   those with an eye that doesn't
    close properly. Those drawn on a plate with a nib
    dipped in blood crimson those in muted colors. Fate
    is simply what happens: ask the Greeks. I am the Jew, one who works
    hard binding wounds.
Ice circles melt to drinking pools.

St Francis' birds drawn mystically, filmically, hands the template
for all that is drawn
in us.

Suck your breath in.
Beasts are pulled thru cloth in the Bayeux tapestry fox & hound:
Blood yron tinges them
In the Flemish Unicorn tapestries
the albino circled unicorn knows neither encircling or salvation.

Give them water   clean sky for nourishing; Wearing that coat, I
look like a Dalmatian going to a fire:

Ishmaels, they will leave your palm, exiled, moving on in a pilgrimage
daunting lean
as licked bone.

What animals came
to the burning of the peasant girl, her hair unknotted, cut in a shag, a bowl?
What animals came to the sinkhole in Kentucky after the mother deer was shot, the yearling? To drink blood:
Over & over when the flexible sad animal of your body came to mine for bending
& all I could was hold the stiff white board
what love came to nothing.
Not anything, a pool like the golden swarming the bee makes around himself
What beasts to the immolation, the cremation?
Not those who timidly made circles & ovals of water with their hooves those kind-mannered things
I stopped talking, looked down to the wood table
I knew a trick of almost stopping breathing
I didn't want to tell the audience what happened in this <u>special</u> story
an Afro but blonde shadowing the wall opposite me I averted eyes turned them down
like turning down wicks on winter evenings
dropping an anchor in a miniature world
turning the setting slighter on passion
It was immense moving, how I made the terrible choir
of entering the hive one day.
Half a century later, the miracle is still unfolding the magic is in how like children lined up for toyshop opening in tiers, in tears
the story
unfolds
& how the bees, like the lucky horse on a carousel, keep stopping at the honey
just on the money.

Frost on Roots

Pilgrim & Pinto
Have gone ahead to search the countrywide, to scan glacial ponds
For the bride.
Here is the shimmering pregnancy
The monk with crosshatched knees
A baby peacock is sent ahead cardboard box with air holes that make carton look lacey.
Graciousness a whippet, a greyhound-swiftness driving him
Follows close on the hind.
The bugle unwinds gold notes without a thread of blood in them.
Not yet.
When it dips to twenty below, air will sear lungs
Their footprints will be buried in snow tombs
All except those birds, which fly leaving only wind, beats to scar, imprint the air
Leaving, till sunsets, swallowing all
Their immaculate shadows seamed in & under glacial ponds.

When the waterfowl put their heads together

When Lo says the sparrow hawk
When the owlet's head turns 360°
& conveys talk
when each & every sound startles
like lit paper—shines like cellophane
or the slipcase, silvery, of the newborn:
then, when sun is yellow as your five-year-old's slicker
(back when you had a celluloid tub duck & dot eyes
the whole bath smelled of old rubber
the war was raging
pipes crisscrossed like lace everywhere)
dying chicks kept on newspaper in a wooden box 2x4 under the kitchen stove
back before you lost your legs
& folded them away like striped tights in the next life you'd wear:
oilskin & ebony boots in which to go clomp, clomp, clomp
the way the morning & evening train hoots:
then remove slicker, take off overalls & shirt, last yank off boots
go pure as the starved wren thru icicles dares winter fruit.

The Brightness of Toy

High   floating above the municipal pond   the brightness of
toy after a night of agony.

A dictionary of toys: that's next: an anthology   starting with poems
praising Bright Apple
mechanical toys:
wet-black wheels
a boat with yellow paddle, celluloid duck you could punch in & dimple it
like an oil can.

Back of us all is a windup key.
gold-plated numbers for night   glass numerals for day
one cannot count penury.

Childhood's dark disciplines
Sabbath whenever it came.

To be a child with an Iron Lung by the bed on the Fourth of July

Like potatoes,
These were eye-root-growing   limb-lengthening days
Poke in the belly like the Pillsbury dough boy.

Deflowered, now I was twelve, now thirteen: white pills were ready as
soap in the blue night coming.
There were sombre
I left behind dolls who became deaf-mutes
some lame bent down, some ascendant like a ballerina's chignon.
There are landscapes that can break you like language
In morning
the soft green eye
broke open   in *agon.*

Over my head
floated

the Chichester psalms.

Geoffrey was moaning.

I banged my heart like a drum   but no one came.

What remains
a mercury landscape spilled from our drab suburban yard of that mock castle home
over my toes and   fingers losing feeling then   voice ragged with screaming:

Mute
with outstretched hands
looking Mutti straight in the eye "White Lady's a street name for cocaine."
A child must give her *full & undivided attention*.
Toys darkened. A clay glaze fractured across them from the kiln.

In morning
the soft green eye
broke open   in *agon*.

Over my head in the ward now floated the Chichester psalms.

Kingdom of toy now moated

Shiny raven brushing my cheek with terror
on a village street   driving the medieval spike in:
Dreamed itself on, like flour kegs a winter afternoon in Massachusetts
        or rolling pins.
World, I interpret you as blind. Unkind.
Childhood's towns burned to wallpaper towns: a placid Pastor, some lowing kine, the peaceable kingdom.

Audition

       A down East thunderstorm   against a land clean as hog's
head, dog's bone
       breaks over saltboxes Cape Cod.

       Spaniel listens. Horse glistens
       in whipcord bleached light
       They are auditioning: animals for eternity.

       Houses
       nailed in a blue bottle glass bottle
       wood like spider webs, lace

       ships, which sailed from Europe
       arrived with rising sun
       Almost drawn in water

       The light of the world which shines
       From cracks
       Do not fall between the lesions.

A marsh hawk
raises the pulse:
fluency, riding the wind.

Saltboxes sink, refuge in a study, work the years may wash away: dark salt
lamplight-lined golden
in a cone of snow as golden retrievers temper in their coats fiery,

       Dead bird in a rocking chair.
       Sunset leaves a streak of blood up sky.
       Day a single black Braille dot on winter page of sepia, pearl sea.

Braiding her hair in morning
knuckles were white.
She put her hand to her right hip.
                She looks like an albino hound in the swing-mirror.
For a long while now she had been aware that pain is sexual
That it cries like a babe for milk for tenderness.
The dog, Arles, thrusts his snout from his kennel, fur outlined in frost.
Was he among the found or lost?
His tail was too frozen to wag but Arles perked up as she approaching her
braids now done in a bun.
She was lifted, she entered other spaces after a shot for pain.
Going on photo shoot was more difficult for her now
Still, she rose as if to meet her lord, or her love
Rich with familial love
To the view from the back porch up there in the north woods every
morning
Like turning the page of a revered book, some family album,
To the next page
Illustrious, rich in decades of affection even if it was the album of
Misfortunes.

Misfortune sat at her table in its lace & linens.
Mrs. Jolly was opposite
Blotting her lips on her napkin with the first helping. After the second a
belly laugh filled the room like a new weather entering, tiptoe at first
Then like a whole funeral in home letting abundance
After the sufferer, no longer among us, the soft animal of the human body
slept in bone fine as elephant tusk ivory.

Mice who have been to the fine arts museum in Boston
you have seen paintings thru glass.
but returned to a close-up of grandmother newly in the asylum   from whom
you cannot sweep away lifelong depression, with a pirouette or your dancing body nor
with a straw stiff broom.

The porch outside the pavilion still has leaves encased from autumn:
maples scarlet in ice   like lights in jars:
Her grandmother's sorrows
she sees as spheres of oil in
burning.   There is no genie she can coax to heal them.
  This is new, the psychiatric ward <u>at one in a</u> January daybreak
    a painting behind glass but not safely enough roped off, you take
    photographs of, make eidetic images before you   once a frail,
    shatterable girl,
     laments, on a Jeremiah morning, before going with her mother
    on concert tour to Japan. O now Nippon.

Federico's Lamb

i.
In a wire basket poems collect dust diamonds:
The blown box of the world gleams.

Kitchen window filling with pearl snow:
Federico's Lamb in the bath window, blue soap in white sun.

In North Carolina, they're getting up breakfast & in Asheville, in
Penobscot, Maine:
In the Bible Belt & in the plains. In Nebraska, boiling neck bones of the
lamb for broth.

Home, sky's the color of barley:
The tongue moves quicker than the brain.

Time for the translation out of freedom into work.

ii.
Tallow curls thin to spunglass.

Sojourners canter in wind which sheets their bodies in layers of ice
Making their own music.

One blue window covered with plastic in Rome, Georgia, sheltering
Federico's lamb
Head scrubbed down to a nugget.

Curls come, the kind only pencils sharpened make.

iii.
Trouble renewing passports
Moving back night like a panel over a painting.
It isn't debt alone
Apart from that debt the world exacts & never pays back.

It's distinct quiet makes for the sombre mood coming:
These poems in a wire-basket collecting dust-diamonds flare again:
The blown box of the world agleam.

Your Nature Exhibit Box
is wood, contains 20 glass compartments,　　　　　　　each with little
lid:　　　　things hid:
which all will come to light one day

to God:
A cubicle houses a fractured robin's egg,
One, curls of bark　　　　　another a nail.　A snail shell.

I remember Hospital winters　　　the East River elbowing North, striking
crystal hail.
The leg of land out to Long Island shadowing in
twilight

Coming with veils
like a child pulling blankets to his chin,
a girl taking First Communion.

　　　　　　　　　　　　　　*

Wood shavings, feathers, robin's egg　　　scattered like shrapnel　at the
big bomb:
　　　when Elliot spoke his opening line in the brown waiting room that
autumn, he was
close to curtains.

By day he climbed
a hill like
Sisyphus to begin again each morning.　　Many years? 16?

Each morning　　patients in sepia on old brown
sofas　　bloomed
Ashtrays spilling over with feathery ash. He drew the sash, light cut his
eyes.

      Flicking out the light in the blood: he wore his hood:
discipline,
    I bit down
    I harnessed the wind   an eidetic
Small Sistine rising above me, swirling colors lowering to touch my back
    with angel's wing or human hand.

The Six-sided Snowflake
the brown dog trotting   out of Painswick
paws sinking into snow   which will
erase him, pale as water
& us drifting in our pasts as though we wore our parent's clothing,
         faded, out of fashion.

Elated by cold
I unbolt the door with both hands.
Grateful for the freeze & a cinnamon drink inside me. Painstaking,
                       exhausting my mission.

I move forward my shadow   taupe dog, *Depression*,
in two Six-sided
flakes
of the
lace curtains billowing
sugar-dusting streetlamps:
The empty beauty of snow-covered streets reminds me
of Tallin, Estonia
St Petersburg's White Nights.

My mood soars. Something will come along to nip it.
My girl was calm as I was excited.   Now no sign.
A single glass of raku in yet one eve more empty teahouse.
I pin the organdy curtains where they tore   like a bride's tattered
gown
in Mexico or some dusty land
where it has miraculously begun snowing.

The Long Brown Body of the Street is Dying
Like a shot hound   the flower shop in all its colors
gift shoppe
hairdresser

who will carry it out into summer?

On a gurney

Buffaloed I think of winter
when flames quiver, a nest of wrens
& our baby Fragile X was rounded, like but sweeter than a bee.

Portraits go dark on Audubon wallpaper

Elaborate in light as a William Morris print lining a six-sided hatbox.
I rise, a *Dies Iraei:*
Light moves slowly photon-by-photon. The bird from skeleton begins
arising.

The boy hands me a blue yo-yo
a silver wand:
One morphs into a glass ball, its milks clouding.

The other blue-stem roses.
"I can give you quarries of thought," I whisper.
"Hush," returns.
      Albino lace turning blue while the dog of evening thumps its tail
like wings.

Black Swans, White Swans *December 31, 1998 (New Year's Eve)*

Someone always burns the evidence:
the journal kept while the lover was in the Arctic,
childhood diaries the year I caught the virus.

This world is not drawn & divided by Euclid.
While you weren't looking   winter came.
Everything froze: canal, trees   fountain: the window's thin
brown frame is jammed.

It's torture or torchlight.
Only one swan black as wet ink
glosses the skyline.   You've become thinner.

Alarmed   you ask for your silks.
The library lights down the hall click off.
Visitors are gone.

The sky is a black hood. In the painting above your bed an angel's walking;
what is that circle the angel rolls along? A plate?
Not a hoop. Not a fallen halo.   Wait!   It is—

A millstone:

Was bread milled with it & baked in an oven only yesterday morning?
She too passes exposed stone roots. . .
        Winter sun burns
            a ring of
                    fiery minerals without end:
                    the color paint makes
                        in certain oil paintings.

Burst of Sparrow like Gunfire

                      Entrapped, you flew the coop again:
Ash gray clouds rolled up & down Government
sparrows released
by a spring: thirty golden bullets
from a cartridge belt,

"I have the mind of a child," smiled over lamb-sandwich & tea:
meaning she could get *inside*
a child's mind & walk around.

We were winding down, *Sister Donkey, Brother Pilgrim*: scuttlebutt, *canon burst* of sparrows departing underbellies lit by bronze sun.

Like old gold antique clock—numeral-by-numeral,
Red Fox swished thru autumn: Roman medallions, two women:
I brought you home one translucent, bone shoehorn.

50th anniversary of *Krystalnacht*.

No words when it comes to Lowen

For months before she died, *Liquid Oxygen & Sleep Therapy* van came round to Bergie.
She remembered the whole sky in flames
as though every flame in the universe were lit, every tear cried, fleeing being quartered in *Terezin*
a musician conducting with her eyes when the lashes were singed.
Peripheral heartbeats,
there's steady snow falling: upon beast & best of humans:
Look back at that scaffold & black tarp blowing, raven's jungle gym.

Danish Geese in Dutch Museum

        Behind glass in a Dutch museum, the young tour guide
unfolds notes in his hand   pauses before 2 porcelain geese. Hans
Christian Andersen's
white with orange beak.
Streets of Delft unpleat.
Silence. enfolds him the way calyx holds flower.
Rue Marchand becomes parchment crackling under his voice.
His hands have a few burn scars.

At each sentence close, he pauses long enough to let sun sparkle in
thru a Dutch door whose upper half holds cobalt evening:
canals at street tips throb like temple-veins.

A Pensioner

              I don't want to become a walking medicine cabinet
See my violet glass knobs—shove the Dutch door open & find
A Blitz Diary on the cathedral back chair.
"Don't Forget to Write" always near. *The True Story of an Evacuee & her family.*
The panes of light on the bath ceiling shift over the course of this autumn.
A faint pale silver steam-drawn, like the unicorn:
Salt molecules in the air. Snow days are over the top for a family.

Winter on retina & iris
Like a bullet, love's ire when it strikes:
Infantry press thru mud & mire: strange animals etched by December stars:
Then there rings from fire to fire
Adultery or Chastity's choir.

Goose-White, Moon-Bright

parishioners   congregants on the lawn.
Brick pink as a pig
Sun down-dying
Sky soft as a feather-duvet silver & sewn:
To the last rose of summer ash blond
A rose, ash blond.
Couriers, pleading for portage we long to be:
How did you learn the rosary, I ask my friend who takes multiple personalities on.
When she was Moira McQueen
& saw more than one slaughtered lamb in the children of the classroom who taunted her "Psycho!" Lo, O the ride in the yolk-yellow school bus into doom.
"From the radio. There was a program out of New York every day where a priest told the beads and I used to listen to it. There are actually only two prayers, the Catholic version of The Lord's Prayer and the Hail Mary."
I see the dial brown as a giraffe's tall neck
The ancient Philco on top of the icebox in our kitchen:
I pictured cribs which sheltered sheep
In the pharmaceutically-glass & miniature radio tubes.
Nothing was mystical like them
Transporting me to another land
Opium dreams
Pipe dreams, dearest of the deer

(Thanksgiving, 1951 New York—2010 Canada)

She loves her animals
        She brings them in for night from fright:
        after her long flight home before unlocking the cello
Moxie the Irish Setter Mimi the owl. Pager the horse is left in the white.

Moxie's locks hair ripples, red water.
ripples thru her fingers
while Miimi's feathers lift like silk, then settle.

Pager the horse
Whinnies in the 1940's wrought iron mews in the barn
With the ecstasy of carrots coming on.

Each animal thrills in backbone
akin to child getting laparoscopy or epidural who has known till now only
spinal pain.

Post-polio, I left my toys in the old world behind to darken in the rain.
Demon of the ward, the girl with coke-bottle green
Eyes, I had been brought home.

I had to learn how to bend forward in wooden wheelchair
fold one skinny leg over the other one with my arms.
A twelve-year-old girl's mouth moth-thin, would have been looking up at
December stars, catching blue-white snowflakes, grinning.

It's a rambutan
You said as I held up the hard purple-black fruit.
I shook it.
Imagine having the shadow of blood following you in the child who slew herself:
Blood-hands, blood-feet each with five digits, & with a spade:
 The blade has come in:
While I carve a corner of this room for sleep, one for writing, a semi-invalidroom::
He waxes of the sickroom burn like Catholocism in a church: votive waxen blues, purples.
I recall making a model of a Lysander plane when the fire was opened.
 I won't be a troglodyte with bed
in an underground chamber, a bunker.
We muster what resources we can here upnorth:
Refuel for a travel, a dawn birth
While trains cross in stations like black bootlaces.
Safe from anything but a direct hit with his wireless.
In May 1942 after more than eleven months without a bomb, they were beginning to doubt a war was on.
 But once again the Hun swooped
With terrifying sad
Suddenness.
 The rambutan darkens in   nightwind beside the fenugreek seeds.
 The child balancing both arms out in black coat is on closer look
one of our own. Go to sleep formal one. The main stay of your wardrobe is back from the cleaners
& if you could love with a passion, where I am concerned, you would do so.
Amen.

Part Two

Aviary Angelic & Aquatic

> *A hawk drops to the treetop*
> *Like a falling cross.*
> *The haybarn is ticking.*

—James Galvin, "On Exploration"

When fish are pulled from the deep and find themselves in the greater light and substance less air, they are stunned. Many fishermen, perhaps to spare them. . .have left a world of flowing emerald, strike the heads of their prey against the deck.

—Mark Helprin, *Memoirs From Antproof Case*

Fish Blown Ashore

How much longer   waves crashing
dark glass? Fish blown ashore
in wind of such ferocity
the fins are stripped off ?

She wanted to be a lighthouse keeper   & that alone.

Will recurrence
become a hand grenade
ripping fingers   skin wrapped around like blessing?

The body taking her into new strange places she does not want to go
she goes
Wheatland under snow.

        Kneeling for a touch of summer in that sombre grace:
        Cloudberries   dog   lilac   sways in the eye
         like glass come up to her:
        by that untouchable blaze.

I am going out
 From the body
To circle round & round ancient hitching posts.
I have heard God tunneling thru the walls of my bedroom.
A little story telling in symphony of psalms.
A snatch of Swedish folk lore roaming earth thousands of years ago:
A fifteenth century bad boy Tyl.
There you go!
Miserable hen growing up in the fifties
Because she was
Five foot ten. Drift,
Drifting under the shale with all those triobites
The logic of the viola
Consolation
 Inconsolable
will I come back to the body?
Taking every last link
Stretched over chainmail shoulders & spine:
Making a hood
From neck down to ankles.
A rising from and revisiting the limbs in limitless thin-silver framed visions
Snow monkeys learn to wash yams in the cold flowing streams.

His Paws Smell of Soap a note catches like a chime in his throat, he chokes
starts again birch-bark pale:
the shadow of the ragged orange
                                        tabby crawls low to the wall
shoves thru webs, rotting leaves
(Bent boy almond-scented
wedges in the boxwood too.) As if all the seas in the world had risen
crescendo, then most silently.
Mice bones, bird bones, flat-nosed moles burrow under the auditorium.
Bent boy hugs to him a small transistor radio like holding a small animal
Freaked with orange like the cat who whispers in Cyrillic alphabet
"C's" that curl feral, gutteral
Christopher Smart's *My Cat Geoffrey* wasn't more round:
From an almost translucent feline, so close to All Hallows, come ghost-
strange sounds.

Hydrocephalic child with wood & metal zoological garden
Got Calluses on his Palms from Wagon-Wheeling
once they put his cart on the bus
he cried the whole time, the hydrocephalic boy ten, holding his kitten.
longer words than anyone could understand.
The crazed jut jug, color of hemp, that holds the wands he collects
has an earthquake appearance
has varicose veins.
it is hard for him to close his eyes moving across the world on
horses
horses with curved necks
he tears everything some days
All things he touches he leaves in the cart: *animalia pasicaligia:* wind up
frogs that croak, sheep bleat, metallic bird sings: pillows miniature
shipwrecks. The whole blazing furious vision up in flames.

Cider Apples

The soul's at her window of flesh
lightly leaning on a green paint frame.

She
doesn't exist any more:

Only her dark wit
bronze

lets her go on the inside of her hound.
She's in his skin.

She walks around the country.
A gull-rain & sun have bleached an old spruce stand.

She sees witching:
the core of New England.

She writes me a letter while she's strapped to the chemo chair
Indescribable fish float in the aquarium to her left
It is night.
The drip is long.
She will, when she gets out, rummage thru her attic for those things of cambric lace
Her mother left her
Neat as a village reflecting in a canal in Holland.
Scrimmage
A pale black carriage stashed with violet linen carries her, black wheeled, thru night
The horse's breath stains air
The tarnish of objects.
The mortgage on her marriage to God
Expires soon.
The carriage has its ebony, India ink black its wheels that
She drew on carbon paper as a child.
Shadows sharp as an arrow now strike:
Conversations stiff as starch. Lace cuts the wrist
  There are great cities & the little citadels of New England towns
Going on down: her stallion is a racer:
Blazingly bright.
Her horse, blaze, makes off thru a borrowed night with her in tow
  Straight up, no chaser.

"Who Shot Phillip Sparrow?"

Something Very Quiet

i.
something to do with birds

something ethereal
a thing extremely dangerous

the mailman's yellow oilskin slicker a map
the only bright flare
on a gray day.

If the marriage was a walking disaster
the baby was not.

*

Ripped paint on chimney flashings

rain beyond the chain fence

poverty of a wheelchair

The Membrane beneath the garden has exceeded its service life.
Leakage into the parkade is occurring
       & water ingress into the interior living spaces is starting.
Continual ingress of moisture in the slab.

*

The baby is giving fistfuls of grass to the ocean
Will green mix with blue to create a new color she's nuts about?
A Dutch ambassador in the 16th century attempted to describe ice to the
King of Siam.
Water became so hard people could walk over it.

Becoming tangled up in the ideas of northness
like the child in the taller grass

Child in fever-fever land
child in whose lolling
smile a day   a sonnet can be framed

in the north
austere
the bone chilling gaze of our baby.

> Her features look smudged like a pastel of a child's face.
> Hydrocephalic at birth
> Would have been better or worse/

She laughs suddenly
radiating warmth like a Scandinavian evening.
Counting losses at 3 a.m.:
graduation
marriage
children
X'd .
I find a line of angels turned to soldiers of lead
all melted down
to X's which glow on & on.

. . .I watch the well-lit city bus glides silently down black streets flashing
Sorry. I am not in service.

ii.
I swear, by my Catholic faith,
I say a separate prayer
for each knob of her spine.

Hands outstretched she runs grass-stain on her chin
white toddler dress billowing.

Those lashes which throw huge shadows
on pale white cheek
outblown.   She is humming.

The music ends   a feather touching earth.

*

Life begins when the kids are grown & the dog dies,

Will we learn   her patchwork life can keep us warm?

Her too large dresses   float on her   swing in breeze as if her body
were shrunken.
The genetic syndrome   nibbles her in small bites
as though she is turning translucent
I run up to hug her   terrified of   disappearance.

She races but does not get there   is blurry as a bee: Slow down,
baby, stay around

What will it be like when she goes on the rag? Falls off the roof? Has her
first crush?
Risk-taking child   heart's desire   slow burning roof fire
we cling
as you dissolve in our arms.

iii.
           Baby, I imagine that the mole-green potting shed at the top of the
small hill
           is a church & strangely enough you go, fall on your knees, pray
           your enormous head of hair a halo
           your lovely body vaguely squash like.
           But the hill-hut is more a stone crematorium.

You are returning from a strange land   no passport   no
Identification.

Given passage:
Moonchild. Wax paper girl igniting
the high
toll
of being born.

One comes back from hugging you
like very slowly coming back
from the strangest dream.

iv.
Hardness of diamonds & steel.
The mines.
The whole gaze.

When the pediatrician lifts you I want to say, *put her down.*
But nobody can give you back   you were never wholly given
even by the doctor
who handed
you to me
on your birth morning.

Points of compass veered   went crazy.

I throw you a bunch of keys to play with
but you don't want keys.
North intensifies.

One never knows
her child
legs moving like one swimming pedaling
"Pedal not Petrol" flashes to mind.

Terminal to a long afternoon
Grief lays its honor down

Sonnets for Cyan (Cygnet—swan)

i.
In the South there was no swan.
    For a long time I lived there, where two sad voices went down to drink in evening.
    Up from "Discount Liquors" & "Duckwall's. "'Piggly Wiggly's" lit neon an emerald in the dust shone   but never bit the dust: its teeth green. reminiscent of water each nightfall.
    This sad device   my engine   like a cotton gin breathing machine thrust thru a Jacob's age of winters, summers, falls, spring:
    Winters glacial, summers red mud running after flashfloods, falls gold aspens Christ quaking & spring
    a riot of color up from the ground explosion an arroyo twisted as a tormented spine.
Sun painted gold leaf my 32nd winter   Gustave Dore. First vocalists of day
like deeper down South where dust was a river & light sanctuary: scrap-sparrows, gained sky an oven compost heap lay
against the shed in that over-lit city: over streets with mineral names: Coal, Silver, Lead, Clay.

ii.
Tattered songbird, Ebon domes unrolled   like canvases over the 5 extinct volcanoes on townships' western rim:
Township in Africa is know as   a ship going nowhere: Jerroll
"I assure you   *this painter studied the cabbage veins.*"
The rat's flight patterns from the trap's ruin.
Bookstores nested under London bridge   we had our "Living Batch" down by "Okies" bar,
gypsies sleeping beneath looked like large ravens in the juxtaposition of Dore:
ice cold ash & burning fire.
    The death bell knell turned into snow falling in pines.
        How Russian. But this was the blue mesa clouds carving hills with shadows like bread

& land over which red ripples of sun molten,
    At the Prado, tucked in among Goyas & Velasquez was a Bosch: Over-activity: it's
impossible to take all in: keeps breaking up attention to focus on this, that intense magnification.
Like life:
Glittering refuse a boy frowning   a woman's tongue scolding   waving like a broom.
All things of earth for litany: a rosary of bone: geology, anthropology of a coin:
war-plants from the air resemble ancient botany text lessons:
the radiation-ruined ribcages of the dying. *Sangre de Christo. Sandia*
    watermelon.

iii
Wale Wale   the water is wide   I cannot get over   the braided Canyon:
    But blood *it's in us to give:*
the red lens   dipping objects & transactions in iron:
the scarlet crimson running thing which sets in motion our breathing machine.

A heat silence hammered down like a halo
a Medieval boy's haircut A chestnut fringe:
Pinto & Pilgrim serving us, years like letters of a printer's tray etched in:
    How did this wren get into the poem?:
    "Desert Ballet School" where never a soul enters or exits the place
    "Adobe Dry Cleaners" a front for prostitution?
4-square Baptist Church
"Snap-On Tools" truck parked in front
white mallow buildings which took a tonnage of sun

& a beating with white whips became like mules driven
in that over-lit world
where we all staggered, irradiated.

iv.
Dust circled our head like ions of a halo   Ice hammered like
spikes a Byzantine Saint:
negative & positive:
plus a faith one could not snap off & on:

    While the air-waves became the only ocean around
    cresting at high tide & low tide: ebbing: lower than a snake's
belly:
    High tide brought us up   low tide washed us out to
drown:
        Broadcast
    like mercy
    manna to the poor in the *barrios*   water to the thirsty
    fuel to the suffering.

The Owl Italicized

in Durer's etching
the older child has taken 1st communion   entering community this
weekend

His god father flew in. His younger sister flaps her hands:
just diagnosed Fragile X syndrome the "X" and the "Y" did not blend
as they should.

 I ask, insomniac like the owl, why language & hospitals have such a pull
on them like mercury:
those hours in a mental pavilion—gave me a chance to think thru things:
the etchings of voices with no window: AND
who is that walking a toy mouse on the lane frost-outlined? on a chain I
ask
now, asked then:
        White winter bark.
        O cool sheets.
        In virgin, ice moon
        I want you back: days over-lit are like the airport flooded by rain
        quickly turned to ice, a continuity of exile
        then the fatal burn
        like goldsmith's mark blazed in.

Christina's World

The light bulb's a high-intensity thinker
hung.

For Christina,
partly paralyzed,

even the colors of light
shrink like a worm.

Flowered dresses match the rising sea.
Her hair is strong reddish, her eyes deep brown.

Years of confinement
smell of burning oil, charred wood.

Fat cats clot her room
and old cloth.

She gazes seaward.
Locks her look back to land.

In her mind there's a lake
bulb-sized

where energy's pent
in an unmoving green.

Martha's Yard

In Martha's yard
things land in rich disrepair.
Standing in a ring the dreamers hold their dreams like circles of
flowers.

The struggle to wake
began against bare
Dawn

worked on through
the lighter hours:
the effort to become more whole

through work
under blue neural sun
of uncompromising noon

is the religious person's desire
to burn without
taking fire

beyond the fire
that warms
quickens heart & mind.

* * *

Typing in late day, I quote
Martha's daughter mad for horses / who falls off horses
"stares a long time at the ceiling."
"Winter-riding makes colors funny for horses.
Sometimes their knees freeze
above the socks are white stockings."

Her father?

"I'm glad
my child has a passion."

* * *

Sister, I've got your telephone number by the bed.
I study out your face
before sleep.

* * *

We have for our evening the deer
who come & stand
frozen against the mountain like sculpture.

We have the char
of
supper.

* * *

Last the dreamers come
boxes of eggs & flowers
in their extended hands / break open.

One dream? Your husband walks clear thru plate glass with his Stradivarius
. . .Barcelona, those tall concert doors without decoy
glass shattering, splitting his cello in two places:

Mystically, at the same moment, (Eastern Pacific time)
his daughter walks thru the glass stereo door
at home.

* * *

Back porches at twilight
hot linoleumed kitchen

are full of miscarried dreams / limbs thin, skin fragile as an egg.

The least word
misunderstood
between lovers can draw blood. In a fine shell, a nest we dwell

a way of keeping God
near-to-hand:
we draw in extra oxygen / at each day's end.

We have to learn to break
the line,
to break the heart.

* * *

Now the dreamers are prisoners
breaking handcuffs
anklechains.

Fog has burned off
to brighten them
braided fingers their features fine:

Fire-baskets glow in their hands
like wax
with wick to burn.
The night train whistles
steelheads roll in, crack across the mountains.
Martha's yard is hard

under bridges over rivers
    we've driven.

Horsefall Slow Motion, Reversed

It is not apocalypse.
Stroke by stroke
it is you
like a great sculpture of twelve years in mottled stone
rising
becoming air blown
all the particles
like a Seurat painting
—ankle to knee
mending,
knee to elbow
clots healing
or undone
the bright knots of ruby in the sun.

* * *

A week before the horses had been sunbathing.

You moving upward from green
earth
in astonishing

slowness;
each tone & timbre
of earth brushed into skinned hand, arm

immensely light & heavy at one time
as if mounting
air

your chestnut hair
streaming before you
like reddish water

making you temporarily blind

till hands find
touch of warm hide, & leather again:

putting the world back in balance
which was curved
in a fastball pitched to crash the globe

coming down
on you
despite helmet.

It's left you with thirsting touch
searching gaze
for an earth to graze easily again;

It was everything over
in a waterfall, a rush—
or else regain the reins, the wind.

Buckled

The spoon buckled & blistered.
The glue stuck to the wrong side.
The map was bent beyond boundaries.
It woke you from a dream, plunged your hand in blue:

Life
aboutfaced when your child rose
with leukemia
and gazed out the window.

The backyard:
its agate shone like a battleship.
It was up to you now to scale the snow
in buckets of shadows

the tin roof beating
in the Arctic.
The Tundra Bakery lit up,
teeners ganging there Saturday night.

As if she had outgrown life, the garment grew too thin.
Your ears were ripped off like jackals' in the wind:
mica.
The sinew & shrapnel of bringing a child into the world.

Quick sparks flew from the spur of the moon.
A daughter taken into time:
face fixed to the wind as to the mirror,
stars for hair. Or the bird plunging in.

Mad Dog Winter

                                white fanged comes near
red fire
in his eyes.
He is half Holbein-child, porcelain
half wild:
He is my own mother's aborted boy
he is a darkness weighing a feather yet heavy to carry
he is graceful as a whippet, a greyhound in the Bayeux tapestry
in his slight body tapering away from his huge head.
Heart-heavy I come home
lark & own
folding back the night. Sometimes they leave him by the sunroom piano
darkening like old spice, like cabinets where straw flowers
in burgundy hues bloom.

Writing by Lightning

        Such strange breathless ocean children watching old blue
oil cans light up
We are pregnant children any moment thunder will crack &
split us open
in iron bedsteads, hard mattresses, a blanket the color of stone
a pillow that challenged slat for hardness & won.
We were told we were a handful, high strung, exhausting, nervy
reported to head matron
        "We need some muscles on the ward!" she bellowed at thin air.
        Memorable   feathers rare as fathers
Who spoke of or to Moses
about these babies?
Some mornings death appeared
Vaulting thru the trees
A very quiet dialogue had reached frenzy:
hushed, pre-natal milkiness, away from home
like in the armed forces of children
grew forte, fortissimo:
monologue first & last
not a syllable
wasted, creature of flesh,
creature of breath

Dark Tea

A black-blond rain-pond a perfect mirror-glass in a round
down from mountains.
Dark tea.

Bark so black
there's no taking back:
no blur here clarity after clarity.

Rare
jet-gold tea:
rich on winter evenings but this is wild:

brilliant mountain flowers
drawn into small space
blooming miniature cities there is no waste:

far beyond the ravages of war
Exultate Jubilate! At last a place velvet smooth like glassy stone:
so crystal that the deer are come down one by one.

We take the plunge

God is our lungs.

      * * *

The riders in the red raft glaze over:
they went before the fall
thru white water. *Night is the hour of Naming.*

Porcupine & *Marmot Crescent*
Wolf & *Grizzly*
join.
Strength flows into strength,
passion into passion.
O Pinto & Appaloosa evening

as God is our lungs
we all address ourselves at the last
to the dust

as we must.
I press
closer & closer to these mountains.

Is there some way rock could do our breathing?
The noise of boys
nails, tubs in the yard—blessing piled on blessing

strength flows into strength
passion into passion
circuiting / there is no end.

The baker's boy energy
the deflowering
our first brush with love up in Harlem, the flickering neon. . .

What to do with the brilliant child?
ambidextrous
trying a girl & a boy at the same time.

     * * *

We are both controlled / & free-flowing:
the very stones
of the yard circle like dirty boisterous children

frozen
in whatever breach of faith / whatever fashion
life forces them.

Horse-back-riding
hellbent for leather, back from the stables, the ginger horse & the blond
one, she's bloodied her shin
her father says again, *I'm glad my child has a passion.*

Animals Eating Ice

      In the Marriage the living morgue, revolving
      around the issue:
      polishing a loaded gun.

      a brass doorknob.

      The foursquare house on the plains where you lived when you were done in
      as a girl
      is beside a river which never is the same.

      Colt-like girl
      in *sabots* two years earlier.
      It is a photo sent casually by her brother who knows nothing

      Glowing
      on the screen   it keeps unfolding
      like one of Georgia O'Keeffe's roses   or skulls:

      A Midwest sky scraped of clouds the way a woman is scraped for abortion
      Empty: intense
      boy-cerulean like Seth's eyes

      a shrubless concrete set of stairs like Andrew Wyeth.
      Yet it does not make her cry.
      She tells him she was happy.

      In the darkroom paper the house comes up in tray
      film is wound
      on metal spirals at its edges bathed in developer in developing canisters: it took this long for the picture to be brought to light.
      OK. Denial wears a sad smile.
      I walk a mile
      in her shoes: the bones of the house are good

>   but the blood
>   is solitude: Emptiness, not plenitude:
> secrecy. Not rectitude. The animals are in the stable but eating ice, not hay.

Diamond, Black Swan, Black Sun, Drifting
Senses rubbed out
One by one:
Candles n a house
Wight harrowing. The dark salt.

 Colors lessened ten shades,
 Sounds muffled in cotton.
I visioned all black windows
Hung like crocuses, crosses
Caverns.
Within, mirror in these deep room
Reflected:
 Diamond, black swan, black sun drifting.

We cannot stop the bird of the past from singing
Unless we bind his throat like a child. Gag him with white linen.

Then
We gather darkness as men gather change at a bridge-crossing.

Black won't irradiate things now.
So I lie on my back

Counting numerals on my ceiling
Knowing there's none to your world

Knowing my sundial's stuck at
Homecoming.

When flame runs
Thru all the rooms of the heart

The toll
Climbs.

Still, I prize this time
While heat beats thru parent * child who rise to a new range.

Dark, gathered like burnished fruit, is plucked down
From an orchard to bring me back to one in the morning

When the child has no bound throat
And the bird of the past is singing.

In nest of your heart
As I mine.

Part Three

Little Bee

(Enclave, cell, nunneries, honeycomb)

I saw them sitting at one round wood table:
Obedience
Discipline
nodded to each other brown pilgrim
one with clear hazel eyes, one nutmeg brown
Crusoe in England
　Letters bound with string:
country bathroom white zinced Vermont sink
I draw a cape about me for when the high expends itself.
Maps on my backbone, maps charting the Yolk bone of wrist
the tension & relenting lines
Was it in slant sun
I wandered into the brick & board yard at dusk, dust as solid as rust?
If I put my hand thru the past which is dust it would come out coated.
There, history rusted it was so rainy
I cannot know every street, the side effect of morphine
but performing letter writing, breathing out, eyes closed in intermission
I see decorum
　　　desire and design sitting at rapturous attention.

Happiness Doesn't Matter

                         said Mother, when she visited Canada:
"We must not look for it on this earth:
                 It always rained, was always October or November;
                     The winds had *wolfen wings:*
                           she got delayed at customs (which was a cinch in those paradisal days)
                     She phoned me from each port:
                     Seattle, Vancouver:
                         "I'm almost there-I'm drenched thru even to my shoes!"

     Carrying The Complete Letters of John Steinbeck, a small woman, powerhouse, she'd descend the steps from the plane:
     A few years shy of seventy,   shy of little else:
she stayed at one place, then another place:
     The Queen Victoria Inn, Chateau Neuf. Each had faults

     The Empress she decided had mice:
but she liked the liver & onions at *Samuel's*, my Jewish mother in this Little Britain:

Blue hour:
deathrise? (These little mounds appeared in our childhood again & again.)
     "They're not scones," she scoffed at high tea, "They're buttermilk biscuits."
     She gave the devil-may-care slap to them.
     Doorknob biscuits soaked in gravy-brought back the misery. (I had the mizzables down in Florida:
     nimble as a squirrel

& could not slow the quickness in my eyes.)
"I feel so sorry for you I could cry—trying to please
her," she'd say.

I re-visited my childhood as I drove her about.
"Don't look for happiness on this earth,"
she said in so many places

now like an infestation of locusts,
or a fine dust
it has settled everywhere:

She left
saying, "I'll pray for you
on that godforsaken island."

Indeed,
I was now ringed by waters,
on a godforsaken island.
And as I drive about trying to please

my heart,

    I see the shadow of mother, drinking French onion soup here, in a scaffold on cobalt air:

*

Twelve years since we've seen each other.
Let Simon sing about a mother & child reunion:
My brain retains a template burned with Mother bending over cognac:

Within hours:

    she is settling like beach sand, like silk & silt on the sunlit graves down near *Island Road (The fresh graves & the old ones):* & the Chinese Cemetery.

The Maple Leaf flag cracks like cannon: pleats,
snaps smartly,
one whipcrack in the translucent azure of this blessed North.

I've married
it
with all I'm worth.

Deep at peace
(but above sod)
not looking for happiness, or any mortal thing:

in this town
where all the British pigeons
are come home to roost:

Heart constant\
feeling
about to head off on holiday, or step off a cliff:

Turning a wide angle
thru a lens:
doing the humblest thing:

Waking
watching dawn
break white over the sill
the will
watching it light the lintel
the will to carry on, be strong

detached

observing

one blue heron, the ancient one, stir water with his beak as though it were a spoon, but *otherworldly blue as the moon.*

Butterfly Collector
with my net I sail over rooftops
emptied out of anger.
Mornings are so dark I touch my Braille clock & think it's night
Doing a tiger jump
The pouring rain is handsome as a hound.
Naked Afflicted. Buffalo girl, sweet soul calico.
Cut the picture right down the middle
Loose limbs.
I taught myself, while I was in love with Lureline,
to bring *myself* over the top.
Early cornsilk snow beats the pants off everything.
I've netted the glass-white butterfly
So moth-like frail, so close to death.
Without eyes, still I can see
its revelation. It flutters against the iron blue mask of meditation.

Triangular Triage took time
many hours moving the Model A into the barn.
Disorder breaks the heart.
When Robespierre was overwhelmed with denunciations and bundled off
to prison,
he attempted to kill himself but only shot his jaw.
The blade would have no clean run
The sound of Robespierre's execution did not travel far. The animals slept
like shadows under the barn, in the mews, stabled but shivering.
All his ghosts came back to haunt him.
I dance with ghosts daily
sleep with them
my shadow pure as little Moll
Flanders.
When interrogated, I will not perjure myself.
My heart is pure I will let go of being twelve years old, my nemesis, my
angels
Why is an uncle always the boozer, the gamboler talking to his bookie, the
one who rapes
darkening the page of his life yet all he wanted
was to get free:
of Europe, of the recent image of gypsies as thief. Mother, an Ashkenazi
wanted to draw the bed curtains and seduce man or woman.
But on stage she wanted the lime-
light of her light
cheeks rouged
heart, soul down to deepest well & bucket bruised: water
bronze-black:
like the moon I say I may go but will come back.

Bee Colony Collapse

Who helps those who have no savior? (Epistle of the Apostles)
We are happy, evenings   even become exhilarated
When the old fashioned cars, the Rolls Royce are parked in the shed
Polished or unpolished.
Returning at Christmas, I went in search of an old bridge, bombed.
Ruins can draw forth fine cadence of language
Clamant words:
       We can look at things nobody else is looking at
Colony collapse:
       Bee deaths are quite common:
A whole colony disappeared over last winter.
Missing New York intensely
Press the hood figure of the Rolls to your slim breastbone
Buildings aslant like ships in high wind.
The elation waking the last day of radiation
Must be like leaning into storm wind
I like color in shoes, would go all night dancing with you
Till silver fogs over
All achieved, captivation.
A Hymn recital
Edgy, cold but not icy
       Fearing the music looking back,
The soundtrack, like a mountain one has climbed
While all is collapsing:
Honey, wax, bees at their most intense drum.
Ovation. Orisons.

Never let me go
Little bee
I know the art of racing in the rain.
I am an intern wearing white touring the guilds & theatres of night
The Guilds that Make Nails
Put on the passion play, the scene of the crucifixion.
The bakers did the last supper
In an Elizabethan way, thinking thru structures & conundrums.
I wish I could begin again
Cross a campus in woolen stockings.
I once gave coin to an organ grinder's elegant monkey
Now see lace bitten into by space, needles
My turn to blush moving outward from ash
As an umbrella opens on a drab day.the background sky, sharp as the zoological days, the sash.

Bird Calls echo back &
Like Aucassin & Nicolette
Each in an air envelope, stone painted by dots.
Einstein's patterned brain, engraved by thought, the tracks a brilliant takes
When racing, when resting how breathe the lungs:
It's all here in this marble casket
Where music thrived.
Clear plastic sheets protect walls from the damp.
What should have been traceable, touchable, visible
Was not
      Bells cut air & sound froze there
Like the shot rabbit with his, with her alarmed stare.

The birdcall like the affection frozen forever against time
Till such time   one can take & rock to sleep the stillborn in one's arms
Singing lullaby as though the death were like the born.

Mystery House

                (in memory of Carolyn Maisel)
    i.
This is the house you lived in when the unspeakable happened.
Fragile as the wing of a bee, snapping off.
        Sketch four walls & a roof half blown
        a textbook child's crayon drawing.

      Out of the blue, your brother sent you the photo, "Mystery
house."
      It is the house of *Sybil*, the name given the girl with 13
personalities.
     Doom-yellow.   The sky behind it is extreme   in its dullness,
ugly duckling: no cloud or tree, steeple nor bird, up sky.

        You wept first in the tool shed
        with butcher hooks
        spades

        the breathing worms
        in cold
        metal cans on chill earth floor. Wood walls the color of bleached
green denim.

        And then you told no one
        you wept
        no more. Leaning over curly green sea, no rail. Dark door.

        I see the mystery hound you rode all these years
        Pilgrim, tall enough to be ghost of a stallion
        the color of link-chain   translucent as florist's cellophane.

        I see the yellow
        map
        we crayoned of Guatemala. I see my imagined wedding

        My veil
        shades of recovery.

Juliet's age I, taking a tall cool drink under a Houston tree

these are the non-negotiable, the unforgivable things.
The most luminous part of the body
The pearl, violated, illumined:

No sheen against the throat of a woman
But spade-shoved into earth:
The corpse of The Broken Man.

ii
I watched Mother strike the Diamond safety
match
I smelled the sculpture in the air

I watched his face catch fire,
curls
in small brown ribbons, feather-like brush the floor.

O light, tight-lipped as a schoolmarm. White-knuckling it every breathing second.
   I found the wreathe-engraved
   wedding band (waiting for absolution or communion)
   in the top dresser drawer, velvet lined, like the casket of the
   greyhound, or the child king:

The wires of faith high strung over night's canyon, the fine wheels of world
   whorled & turning.   Revolving & meshing
   wheat threshers threshing into the blind grain storm.

The girl scissoring across the lawn: A child
half dead with a secret she could not tell:
half brightness the blue piano in the parlor.

Don't store a gun beside a piano

Puritan virtues of silence
violence immanent. Oatmeal sky. Ground stone.

Colonial red redoubt fails to comfort:
in sugary flare
of maples first fall.

Gun carriages painted comfort-scarlet
History is active smoke climbs sky
from the mill on the hill:

All the miles you mean to have gone   to have arrived here:
Anything bearable by degrees: Any time but this hour:
within the shadow of a smile, key this box could open. Tryst be
broken.
Hair stiff as straw
muscles tight as stone
with all you have not told, but seen.

 But it is closed a boarded linen factory.
I have betrayed no confidence, Caroline:
You will take it to the grave
 Sappho's shadow, sung & slain

    Snowgeese fly overhead,
    I have been warned that children think such
rebellions as running thru the streets of a midnight town
    With a dead chicken "shocking."
    The cosmic yawn.
    Will you mention the words, "Love you, pal,"as
you go down into darkness, descend
    Crying to be loved, pretending to be your brother
you phone, 'Hugh hung himself."
    My beloved fox.
    As for my old love, kind & strong with bright eyes:
    your face flash flooded with grief when I showed
you the photograph of ward children: "That was my
childhood."

Snowgeese fly overhead.
Needle-children thread the hoop
If there blood is on the other side
For sake of beauty, rest, and blessedness: leave mayhem alone
Color it
Kiss & hug it goodbye:
Forever bed it
Forever friend.

You carried many keys you married in no conventional ways.
To get to the rooms of the women you had loved:
Chatelaine.

Now, like blue whale, you are sinking.
You cannot rise.
My younger love walks you home to the bed & breakfast around the block.

Blue flecked with whitish gray like marble
You carried the girls.
No boys. Beyond prosthesis, beyond paradise

I let myself
Rise.
Morphine alone won't do.

I spread both hands as snowy owls clock in over farms:
It has spread to fingertips, a fire, a music like that bees make swarms:
Icarus girl will I leap from bed
shattering haloes, of ice-blue winter-at-its truest waters, cobalt feathers &
arms.

Avatar (Apiary)
(For Hugh Fox)

The house of childhood comes down
have we not lived there, brother & sister, an eternity?
Lets go its earthly hold, low roots:
with ten hammer blows. A lung breathe, a puff
Five strokes of the brush
are flourished in my brain
but it is so long ago
color ribbons of bleached wood & bone wood
star the ground
as if earth were another heaven.
Somebody traded old watch parts in
for green circles on brown rusted soil? We are laddering it up & down
darkness: left
alone, behind is right. You examine the Lord's work closely even under duress:
Now I can proceed with sharp strokes against snow
moving always forward, forward, yet backward at the same time
a person on an alabaster, albino treadmill
with gold sparks flying
always marble light making my relentless legs go
night made for walking thru trees
day for marbles, the shape of the earth brilliant jet-greens & yellows.
We have known each other forever....
don't you remember our little place in Avignon? And
how we loved the Rhone....and even all the papal nonsense
that was nonsense theologically but masterful architecturally?
A click of glasses
and more eternities together.
The stage bell rang   *then bluebird sang.*

It would be lovely to hear from you in the old-fashioned way
fragile as numerals on a mystical ledger
the giraffe walks across, tightrope walker, haughty nose high, mouth
perpetually downturned
the opposite of a laugh
End of the fire dish that the animals came to as if it were the water hole
but got burned.
A little floor-heater red as a beet,
shall we build an extra incubator for the 48 quail
eggs over which we've been quarrel-hearted
quibblng?
The fire ovals
of mirrors
hold horses & bear paws; hold
light's levelings & love's laws.

If we speak a river language,
Are we in danger of drowning?
From New York & Holland
Aren't we used to street noise?
Yet there are those into burying the hatchet in the other's back
Fog banks rolling,
A light boat
An amiable dragon
The whiskey circulating
The candelabrum.

Your last days on earth come to me
A forest of birch trees walking
We are now orphans:
cloven.
I whip speech
Small oxen.

Pheasant under glassfall at last
Fall at last:
Foliage glaze
Orgasm's blazefirst time
In a decade

Twin tan dogs, *Obedience*
And *Discipline*
Trot at my heels along with *Manners*.

My red chimpanzee
Sasses me
From the banyan tree.

I polished like guns
My disciplines:
Music memorization

Which I must take to the hospital roof
Over the East River
Wheeled on a trolley.

These cameos come back
Oval
Ivories one-by-one.

I think of
Mother Courage
Smashing the glass which came with her meds

Till it shattered
Out of her life's frame.
Old soldiers do not die

They dissolve.
O brunette
You have stripped life like willow bark

The wand in your hand
While Doppler
Of fog horn pitching warning like small hooves dug in echoes despair so near the
                        verge of the ravine.

15th' Drawbridge

i.
This is the 15th drawbridge skeletal on sky   against
a charred socket of a city.
Opposite,   waves are crashing against north country
A lighthouse is shining   upon   a surfacing dolphin

Will an invisible torpedo go off in your hand
tearing skin   wrapped like blessing?

Since the scourge began your boy-thin body has been taking you places you
don't want to follow
but go   charred as coal: virginal as snow.

ii.
Passchendaele   echoes fall
infantry in endless mud & rain   dead cries of birds   blow.
Feathers.

The drawbridge   pulled up behind,
you look back over your shoulder   to that land
loved, known   :   dark Braille dots rain

Coke furnaces,   lime-burners are black. It was going to be
tomorrow the world.   But a gunfire of disease hits the land you habit like
flak.
Today   Count your money: coin upon coin.

Clear your throat
Cloudberry
dog & lilacs   cry

night
There's a burnt umber glaze   to the past few days:
        similar to the glaze in a dying musk ox's eye:
on your Belgian vase in the parlor containing   a transcending
untouchable iris of a palomino's eye.

Mud Fields of Passchendaele

i.
Death knells
pile
    bodies on hills   color of burnt nail pale
        Passchendaele

A door in the rocking horse   slipped in a small body
of the young Jewish boy   who could have been me:
carried that way from Bavaria

nearly to Germany
But Poland's barbed wire   hooked him:
Auschwitz "Work Makes Free" blazing in black iron. Twisted thorn trees
in Winterset background. hideously

on the iron gate, twisted German Gothic letters burning on crematorium
scarlet sky.

ii.
Sunset bathes this study the color of gold tea   where you have brought
me in exile;
I look at the hundreds of books you've given me:
In day's last sun corners are neat as fine wool blankets   the color of
Dutch blend;

a tea-cup rose curling:
the dragonfly fell in & died.

In dream, I turn and sigh, "She died."

Poems have been tooled like old penny.

Bend sound like our instrument to our will, how can I?
I observe in you a see-thru exhaustion:
this evening.

We are married to water fields which flow
over & about us
liquid as language.

Nights
you brought a harsh message to me   *I know better than to shoot the arrow.*
A Molten motion
sea breaking violet   wind blowing   begins out the window, down the ocean Mud fields at Passchendaele
where all
went to hell.

Never to Forgive

Hiroshima   Nagasaki   Dresden.   Three-Mile Island.
Chernobyl.
the Atomic Bomb Explosion at Trinity
Los Alamos

Carrie Ten Boom
Hidden Children.

*

Diamonded spiderlings hang in our garden
a hummingbird thrums at his sugar water
bee-guards removed because he is young his wings beating like a drum.

> Violated, the girl saw the root on the rose:
> then   took from the world its glass
> radiant as light circling a hothouse:

> Then she took to her flecked eye the ground Leica lens
> the globe receiving
> houses curving like a dancer doing a backbend:
> > neither forgetting nor forgiving   but accepting
> > globe's ambient glow its keen *Amen.*

Boy with Ball

Autumn brings a buzz of children's' voices
a toss of color
darkens ground
a moving shadow
burned by a red fire pump
like the bouquet the bride throws over her shoulder
and who catches it? Who the heck wants a hope chest?
Or bird seed
or wild rice confetti.
Like Boy with Ball
India-ink on oat-yellow
life's spectral.

Here above the 49th parallel
it's gritty, gusty.
Old nicotine light proliferates:
That particular sepia sun distilled in photography studios at turn-of-century
or brown, doctors' waiting rooms: They italicize autumn.

*

Boy with Ball:
Black & Yellow sign
the exact colors of a bee
And he has his sting. See
he's drawn the moment before hand paddles ball:
You think he has it all

but his legs end without feet
Only
yellow ground on which he seemingly runs miraculous like Jesus
or the boy in the orthopticks stick glass when I was young & cross-eyed.

No stumps even.

No War Amp: But a child: And he has this wild deforming: Most times you don't notice. That is because what sign deleted the mind paints in.
Pemmican

Trampled in one of the last stampedes of the century
I lost the lower half of my body: clear as blue glass as far as I could see
scapula for wings   hoof-prints carved in stone   charred in sand.

Woke, this morning to an iridescent khaki
hummer   pleating & un-pleating wings on sky

bookmarking
survival. Gray-blond hay Army colors day.

Reading Braille writing of bark
  swing set upon sky, the soft animal of my body, like a last-century toy.

Why are we thinking of an afterlife?
Here & now bluer than a Russian winter.

Listening to Billy Strayhorn,
that sadfall light
sacrificial song

ice in the pipes.

We pray she won't have autism

while
standing in the crystal of it all
smiling out at us   smoking our hearts out of hiding:

      the Fragile X child
        that extended arm   a seraph carving her fate like sickle-blade
she imitates
playacting with this turning arm rather than her doll baby or brown train:
turning magical
clumsy
cartwheels
over wheat land.

Fragile X

Like St Francis she speaks to the birds.

Her grandmother from Ireland could be her mum   Dad gave her
Asian eyes:
He said to her silent tears,   "Keep trekking, Ling Ling!"

The Fragile X   child lives in a world of her own   a blue
bubble breathing in & out like a lung
removed from the body   floating, reflected earth in its round
azure sides:
hand-flapping   babbling   a plastic bag her favored toy

(Her name means little goddess, or purple flower.)

In wonder, watching her balance her weight, a hoop, in the garden
          a bubble of water
God's youngest gymnast
acrobat hoop shimmering about her hips
her contortions with that water-spine.

Ivy trailing over her shoulders down to her waist, her   milk white hair
Rapunzel
 "Fragile" pulling the bag thru the grass   now with a cream carton in it

high Flemish coloring
high as the sky she pushes away at   ink-blue which covers her like a
cup, a wing.

About the Author:
Lynn Strongin was born in the last year of the Dirty Thirties in New York City and was raised by first generation Eastern European Jews. Her father was a research psychologist who went on to a clinical practice in New York for over half a century; her mother a freelance artist who studied under Alexander Archipenko and attended the Art Students League. A child dramatically marked by the past century with polio, Strongin is often inspired by the confines this imposes upon her. Nominated for the Pulitzer Prize in Letters, she edited *The Sorrow Psalms: A Book of Twentieth Century Elegy* (University of Iowa Press) which was nominated "Book of the month" in England's "Poetry Kit." Her work has been translated into French, German and Italian.